PAT METHENY ON[...]

AUTHENTIC TRANSCRIPTIONS
WITH NOTES AND TABLATURE

MW01130138

CONTENTS

The tuning used throughout this recording is A D G C E A. The relative intervallic relationship of the strings is the same as a conventional guitar tuned down a fifth. However, as in "Nashville" tuning, the 3rd and 4th strings are restrung and tuned an octave higher than usual. In the case of this tuning, the 5th and 6th strings are quite low in pitch. The longer scale of the baritone guitar accomodates this, but heavy bass guitar strings are still required. I first learned about this tuning many years ago from Dr. Ray Harris, a great guitarist and inventor from my town of Lee's Summit, Missouri.

Editor's note: Even though the songs were recorded on a baritone guitar in Nashville tuning, these transcriptions will work great when played on standard 6-string guitar. In fact all of the notes, tab, and chord symbols are written relative to a standard tuned guitar to facilitate the ease of reading. For example, even though the open 1st string sounds as an A, it is written as an E. The notes written on the 3rd and 4th strings are also written on the staff in their the normal octave, but will sound an octave higher than written when tuned to Nashville tuning. It is possible to restring a standard guitar with baritone guitar strings and detune to the pitches listed above. You'll need to install lighter gauge strings in place of the 3rd and 4th strings of the baritone set. Since the highest pitched open string in Nashville tuning is actually the 3rd string (a minor third above the open 1st string), you'll want to select a string gauge that's a bit thinner than the 1st string. The open 4th string will sound a whole step lower than the open 1st string, so the gauge of this string should be similar to the diameter of the first string.

Music transcriptions by Masa Takahashi

ISBN 0-634-06663-3

HAL•LEONARD®
CORPORATION

7777 W. BLUEMOUND RD. P.O. BOX 13819 MILWAUKEE, WI 53213

Visit Hal Leonard Online at
www.halleonard.com

One Quiet Night

By Pat Metheny

Nashville tuning:
(low to high) A-D-G↑-C↑-E-A

*Chord symbols reflect implied harmony. Notation and chord symbols have been written up a Perfect 5th (relative to standard tuning) for ease of reading.

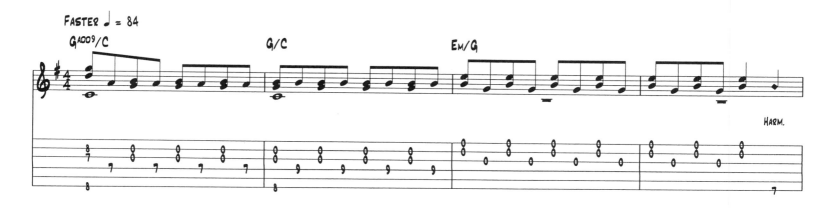

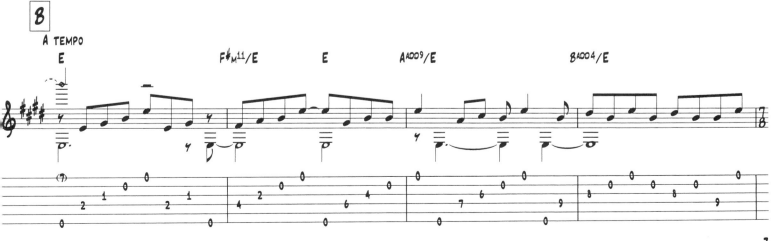

3

4

Song for the Boys

By Pat Metheny

Nashville tuning:
(Low to high) A-D-G↑-C↑-E-A

*Chord symbols reflect implied harmony. Notation and chord symbols have been written up a Perfect 5th (relative to standard tuning) for ease of reading.

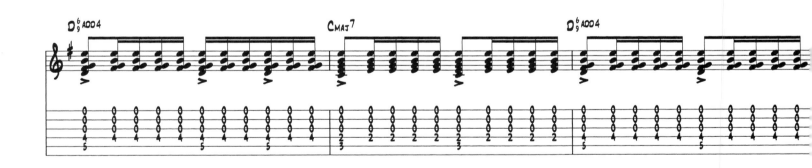

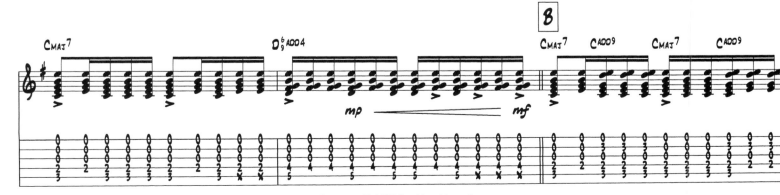

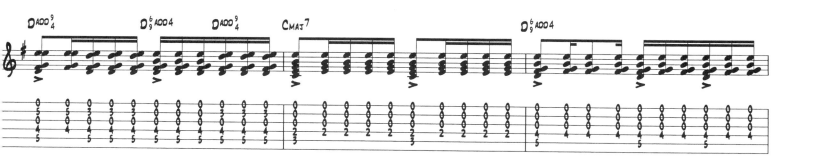

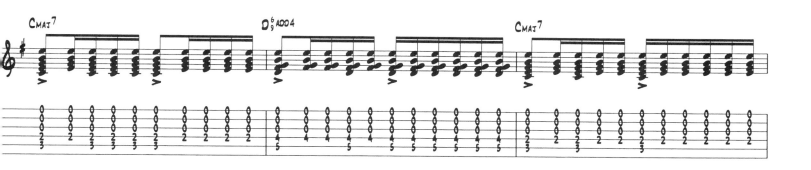

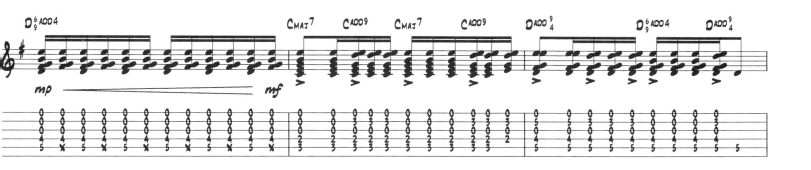

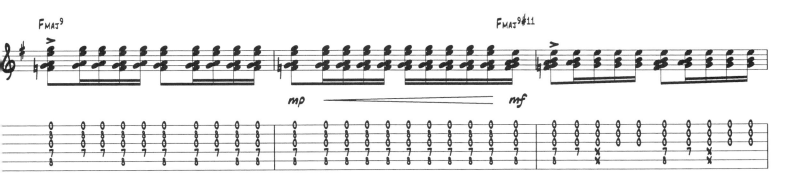

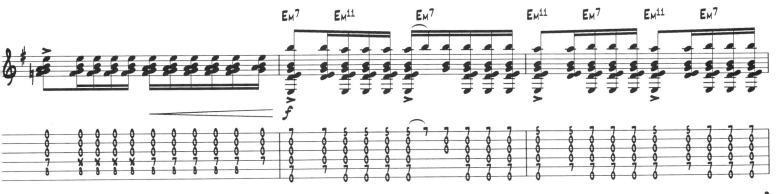

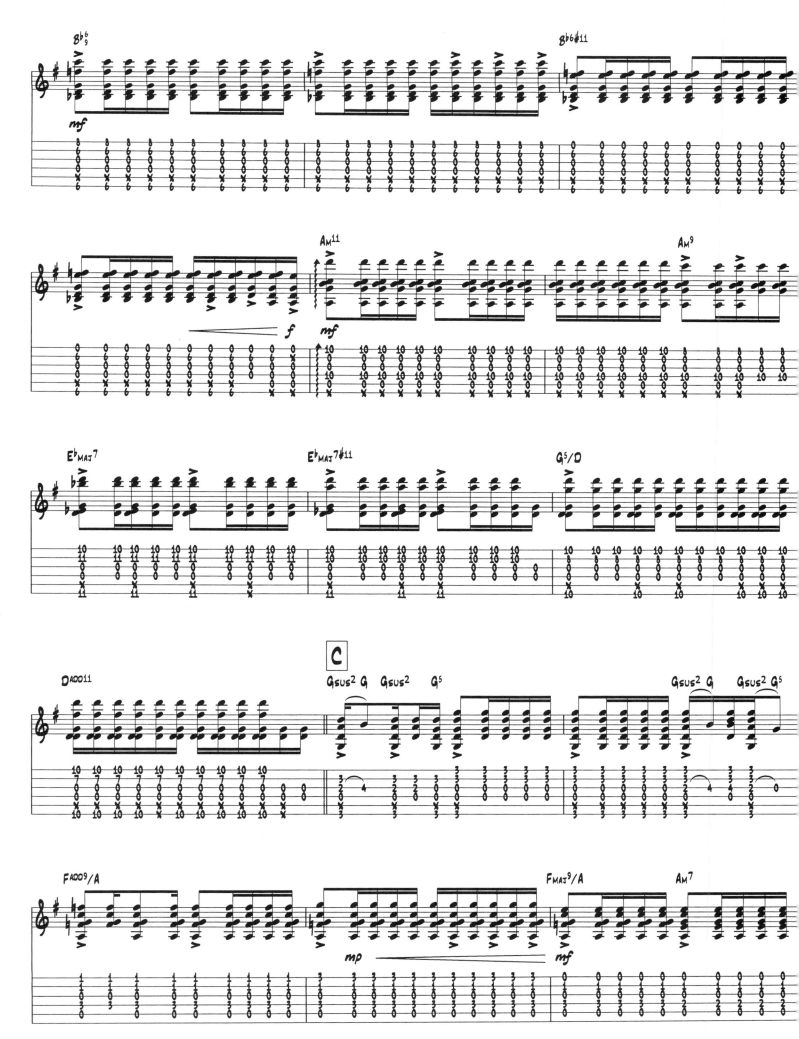

10

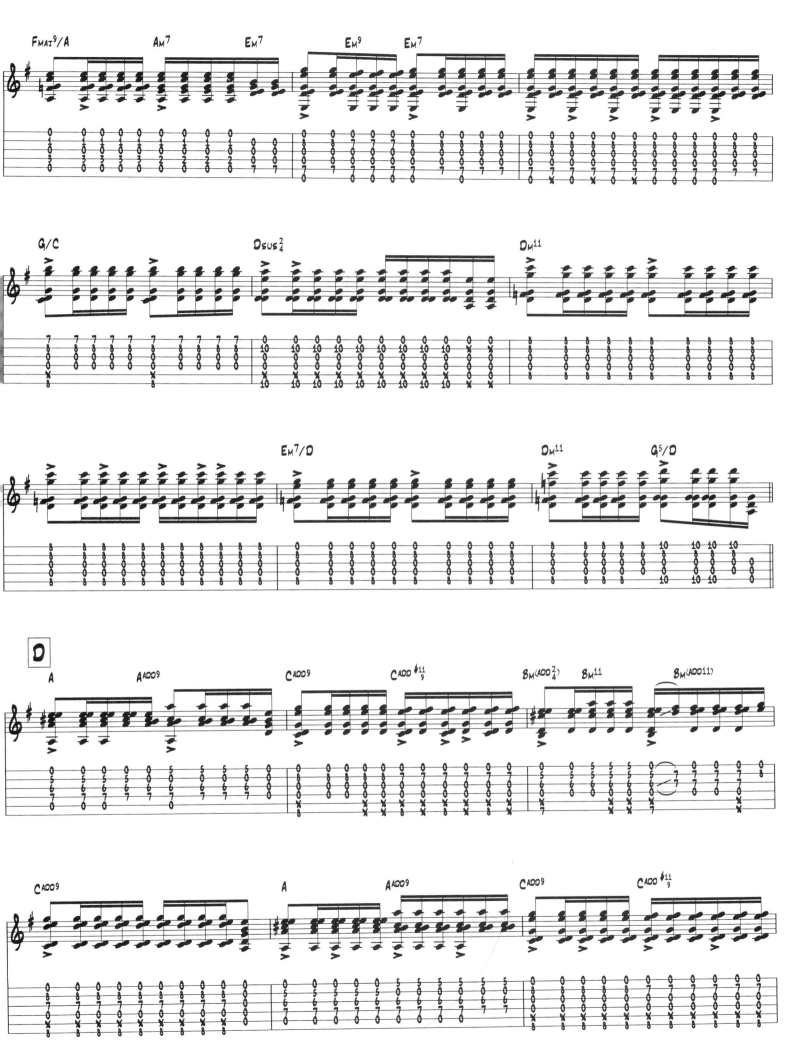

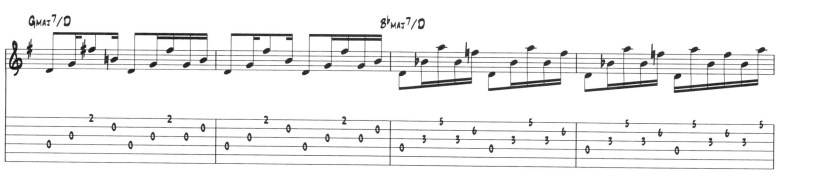

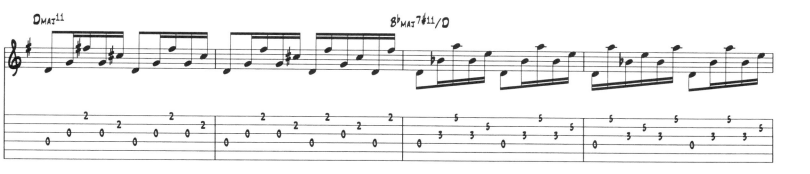

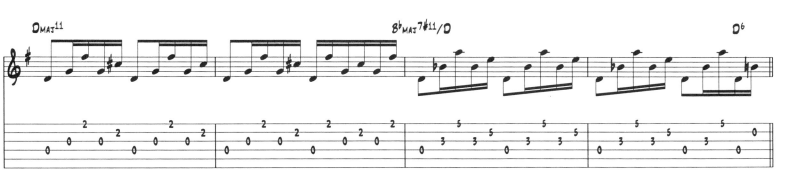

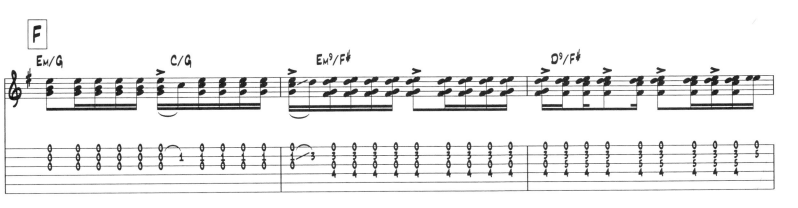

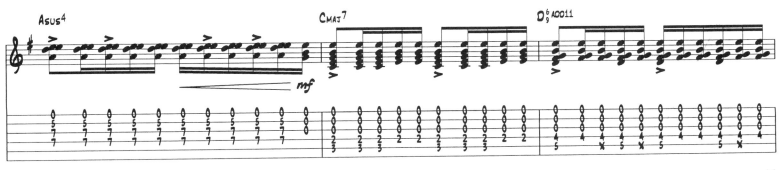

13

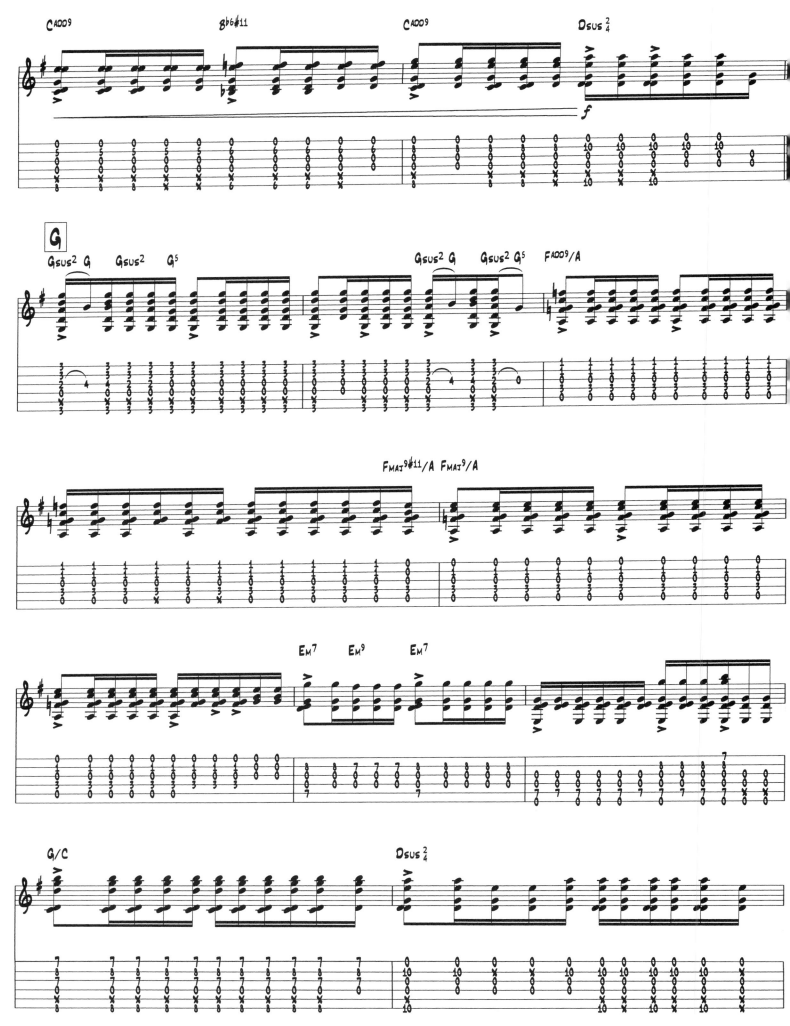

Don't Know Why

Words and Music by Jesse Harris

Another Chance

By Pat Metheny

Nashville tuning:
(low to high) A-D-G↑-C↑-E-A

A

Freely ♩ = 69

*Chord symbols reflect implied harmony. Notation and chord symbols have been written up a Perfect 5th (relative to standard tuning) for ease of reading.

Faster ♩ = 80

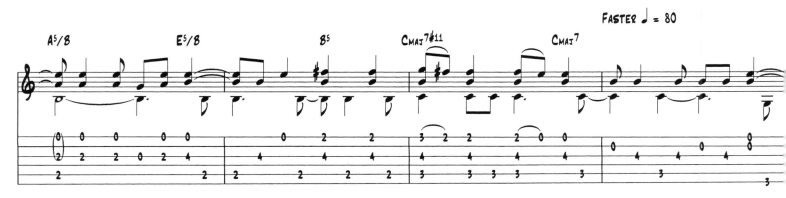

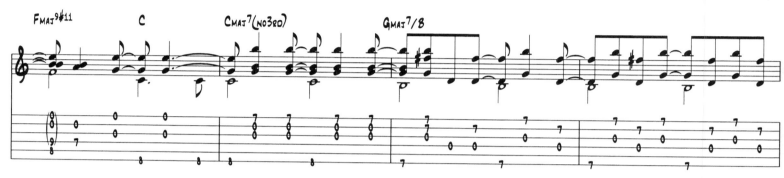

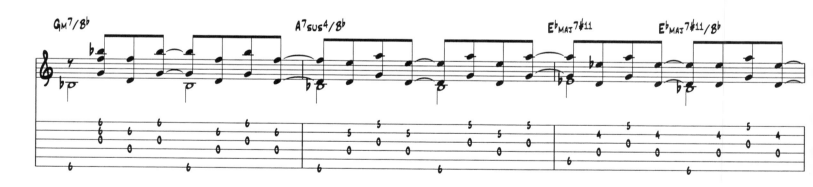

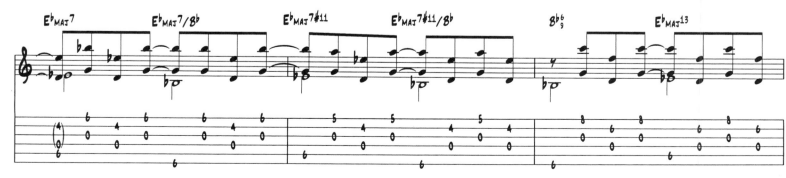

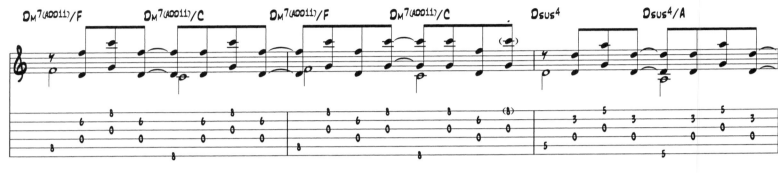

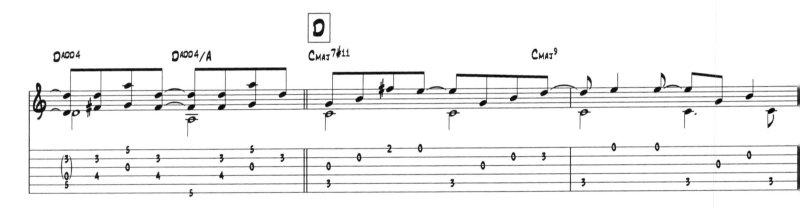

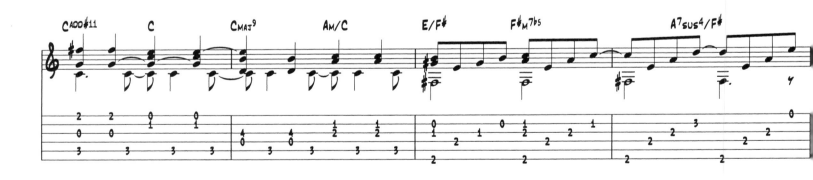

*HARM. --------------------|

*NOTES ON 3RD STRING ONLY.

28

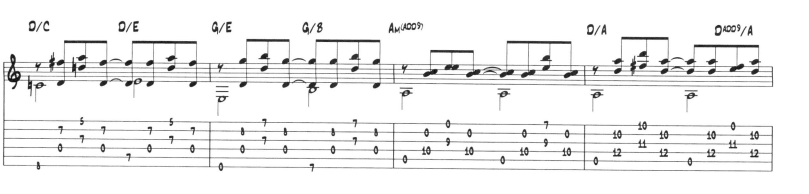

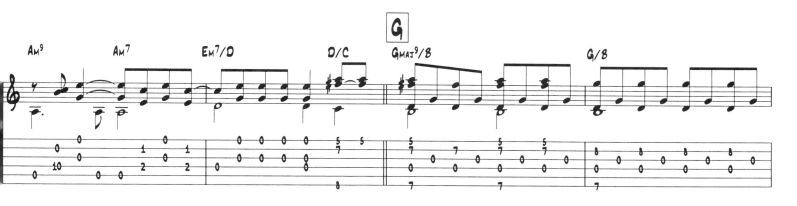

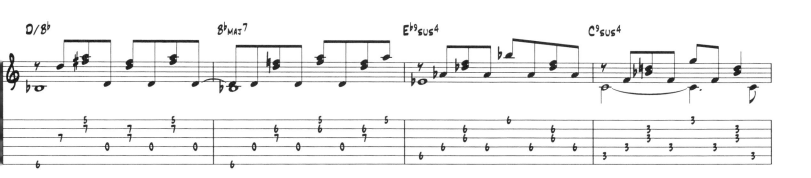

Time Goes On

By Pat Metheny

"Chord symbols reflect implied harmony. Notation and chord symbols have been written up a Perfect 5th (relative to standard tuning) for ease of reading.

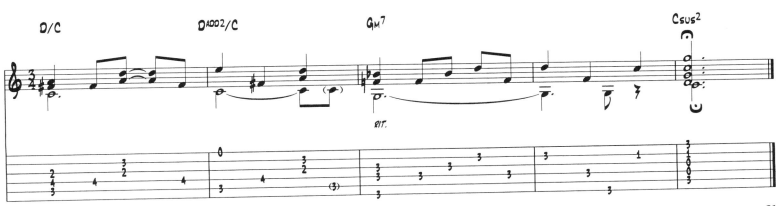

35

My Song

By Keith Jarrett

Nashville tuning:
(low to high) A-D-G♯-C♯-E-A

A

Freely ♩ = 96

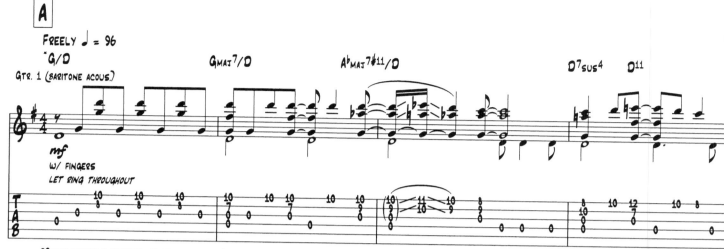

*Chord symbols reflect implied harmony. Notation and chord symbols have been
written up a Perfect 5th (relative to standard tuning) for ease of reading.

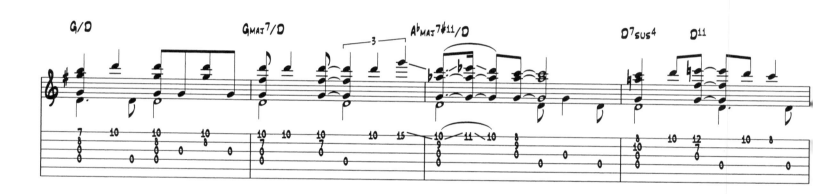

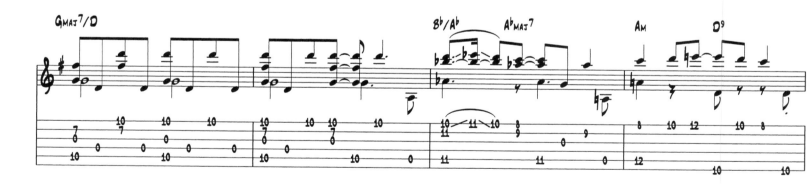

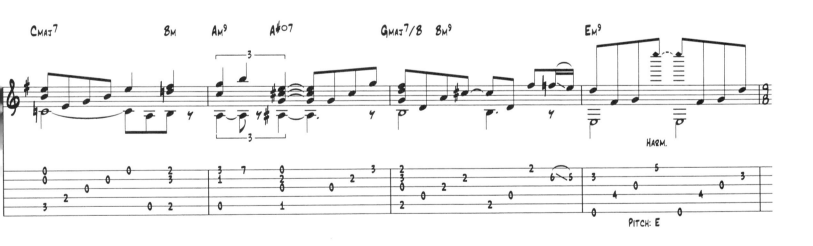

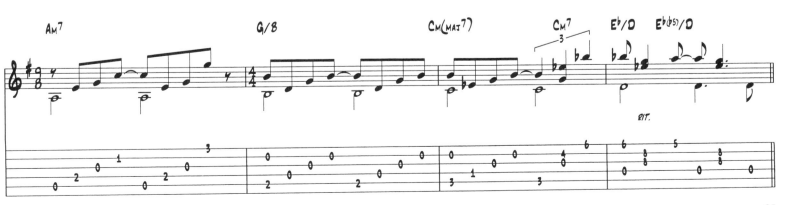

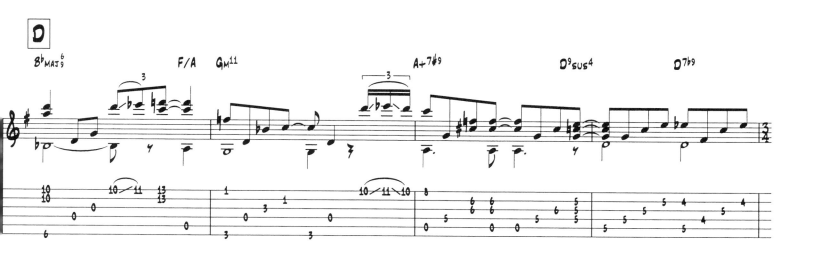

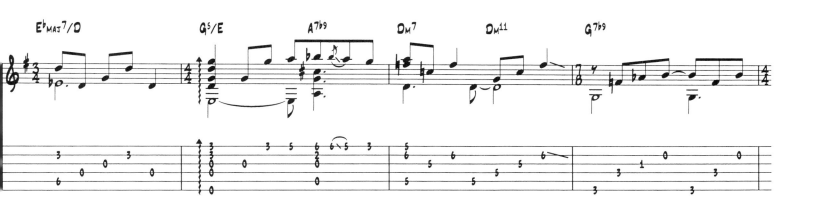

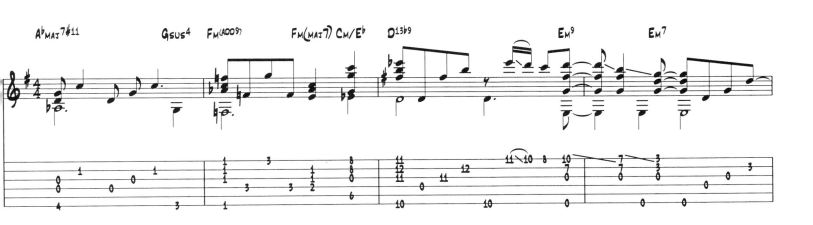

Peace Memory

By Pat Metheny

Nashville tuning:
(Low to high) A-D-G↑-C↑-E-A

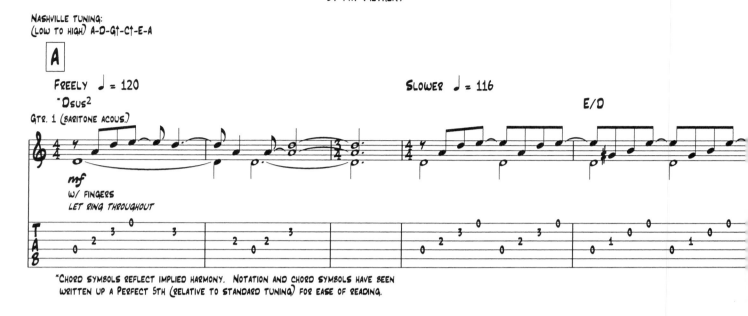

"Chord symbols reflect implied harmony. Notation and chord symbols have been written up a Perfect 5th (relative to standard tuning) for ease of reading.

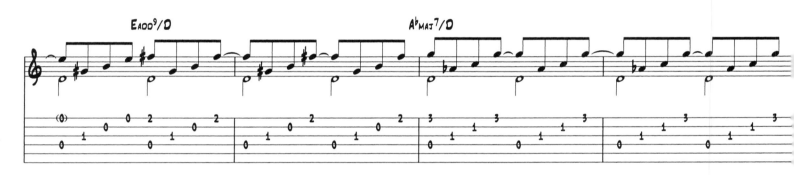

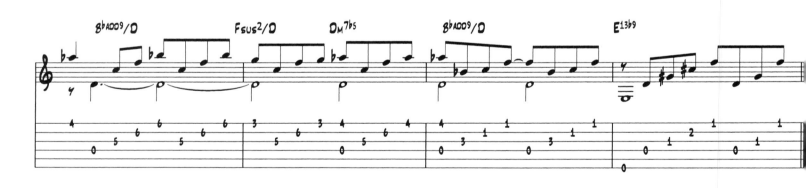

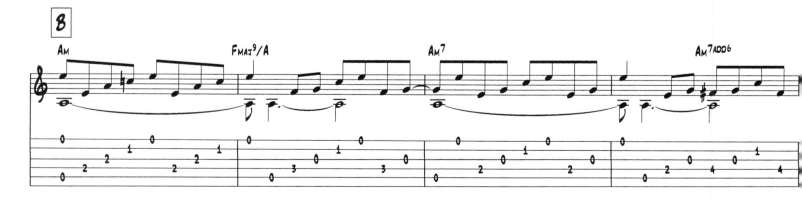

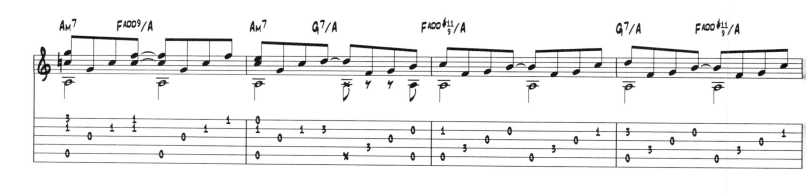

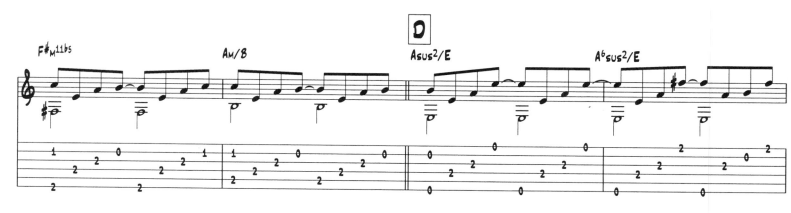

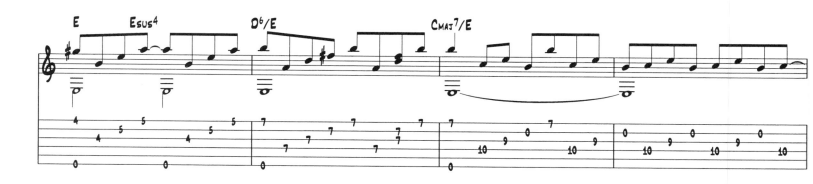

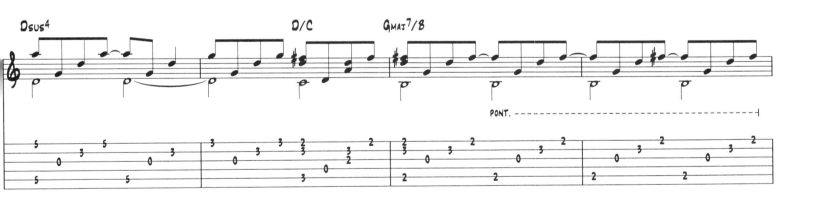

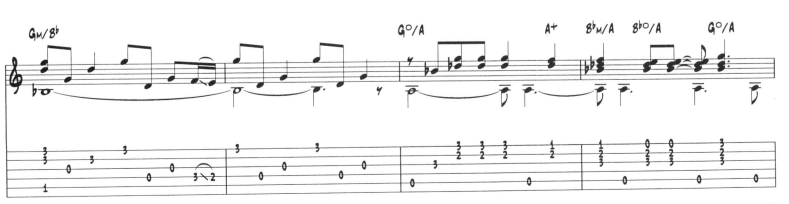

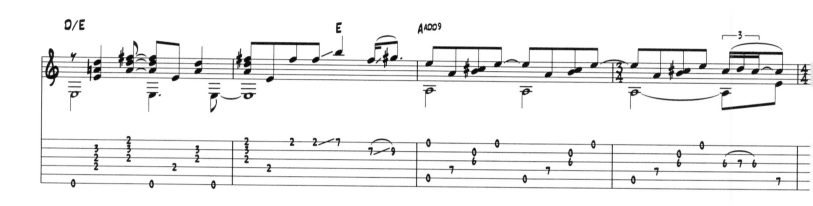

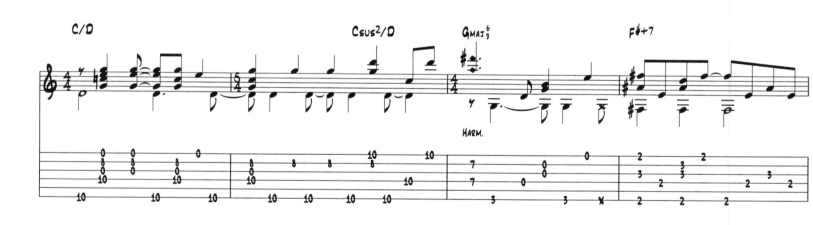

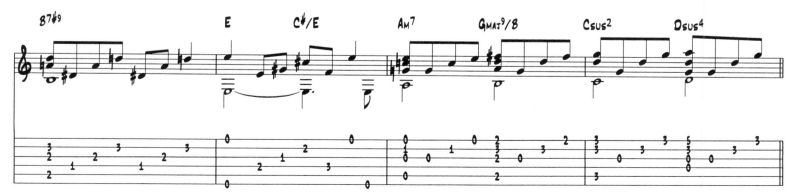

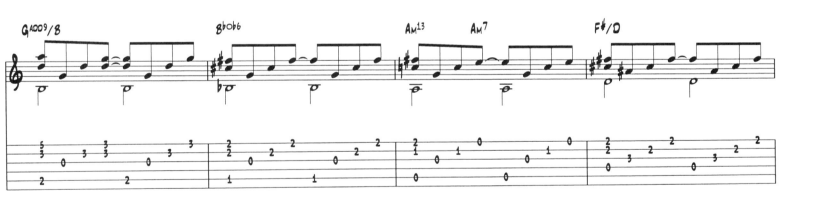

Ferry 'Cross the Mersey

Words and Music by Gerrard Marsden

Over On 4th Street

By Pat Metheny

Nashville Tuning:
(Low to high) A-D-G↑-C↑-E-A

*Chord symbols reflect implied harmony. Notation and chord symbols have been
written up a Perfect 5th (relative to standard tuning) for ease of reading.

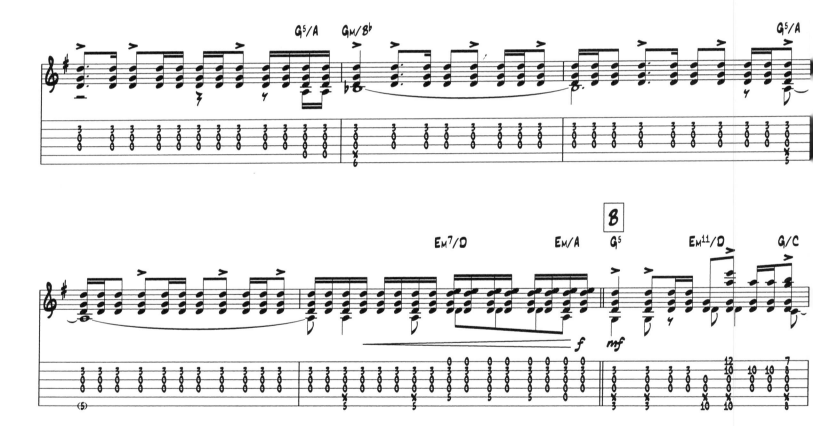

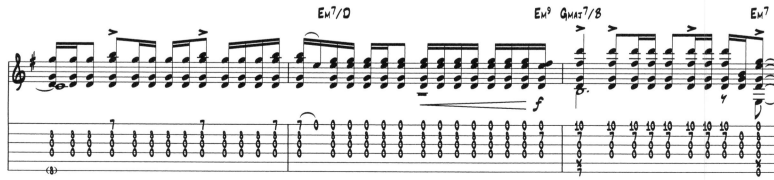

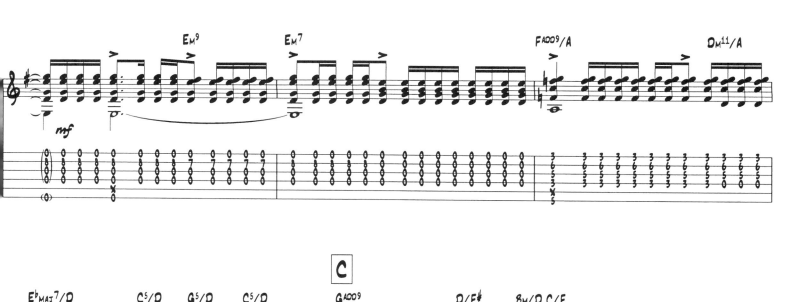

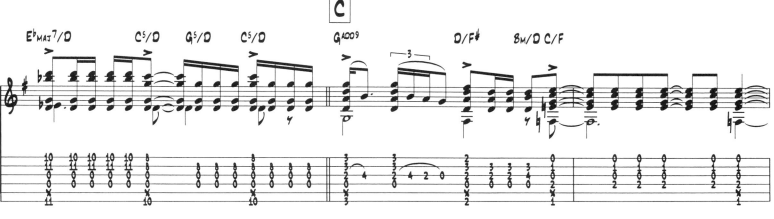

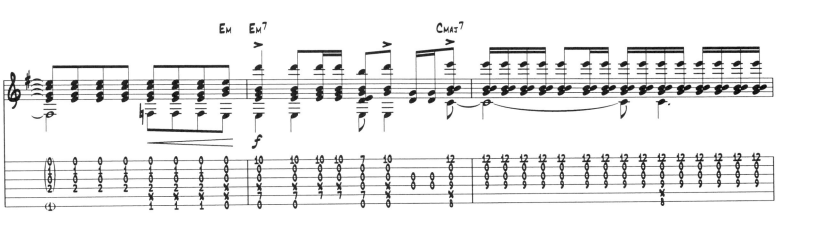

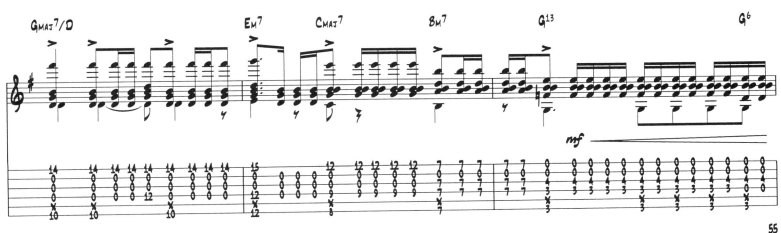

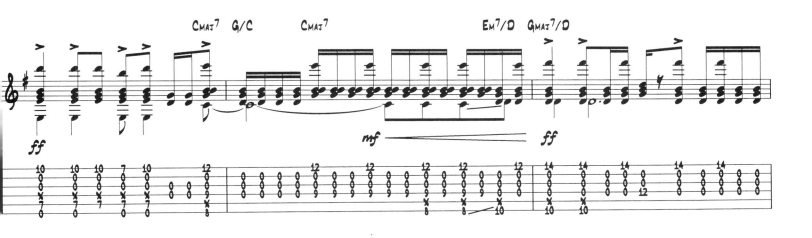

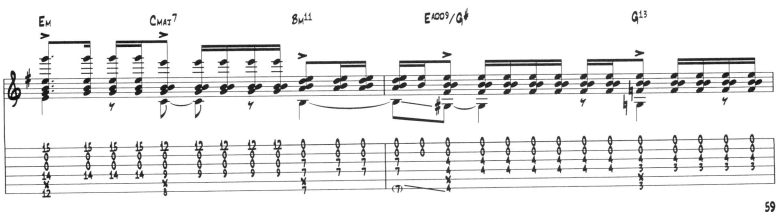

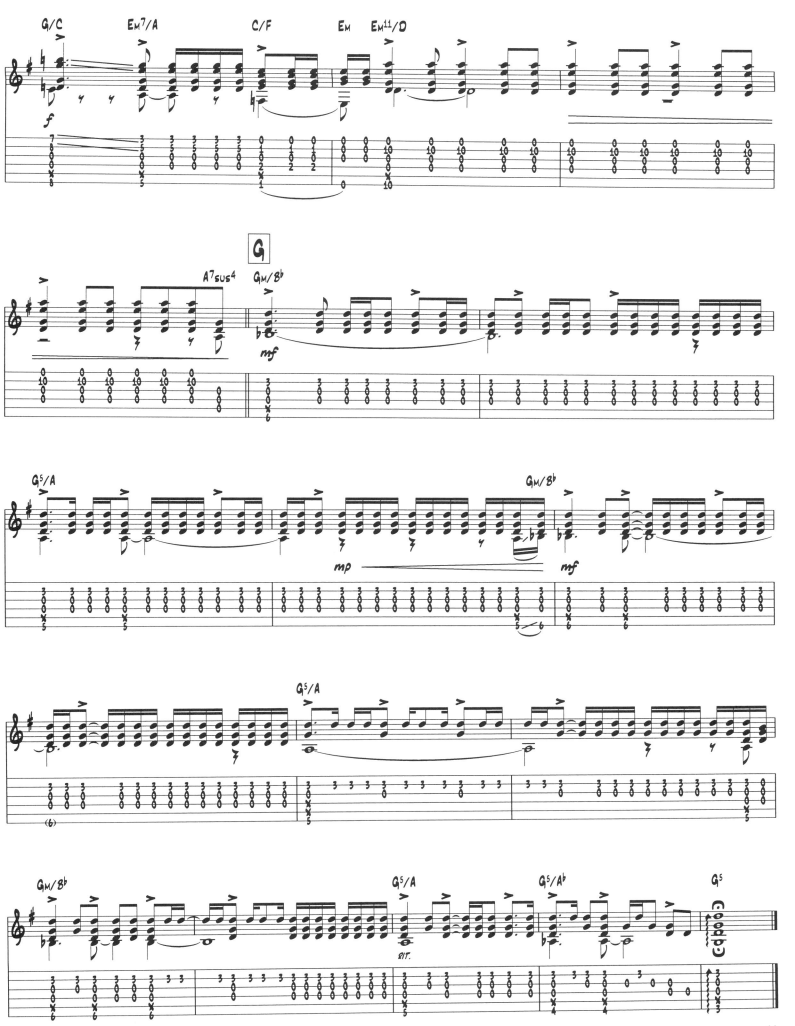

I Will Find the Way

By Pat Metheny

*Chord symbols reflect implied harmony. Notation and chord symbols have been written up a perfect 5th (relative to standard tuning) for ease of reading.

North to South, East to West

By Pat Metheny

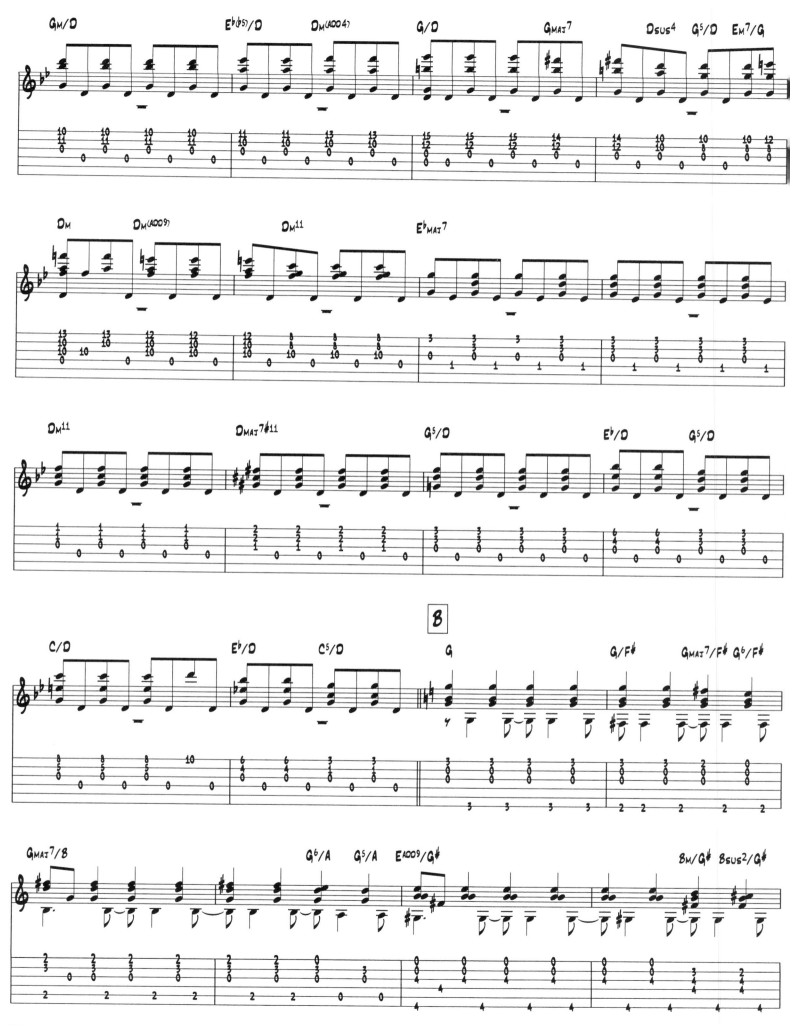

*TUNE 6TH STRING DOWN
A WHOLE STEP AND PLUCK
STRING.

Last Train Home

By Pat Metheny

Nashville tuning:
(low to high) A–D–G↑–C↑–E–A

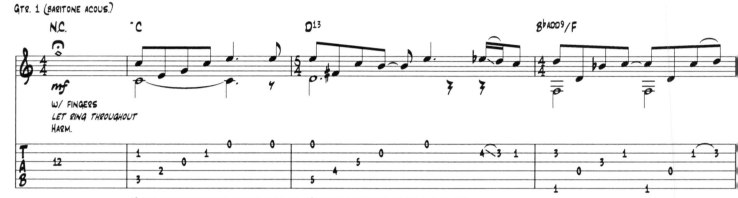

*Chord symbols reflect implied harmony. Notation and chord symbols have been written up a Perfect 5th (relative to standard tuning) for ease of reading.

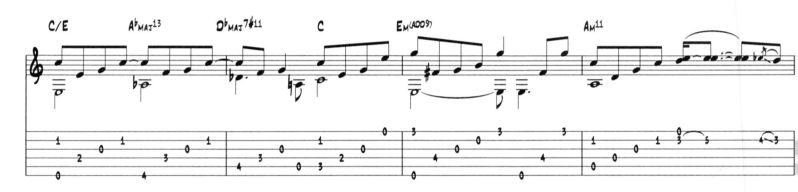

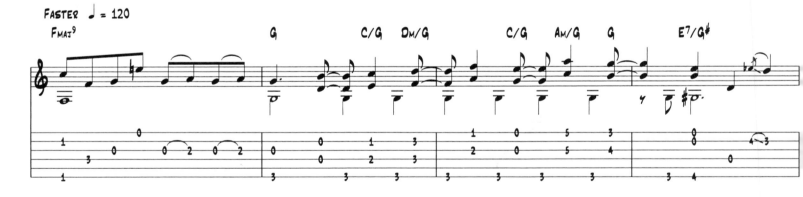

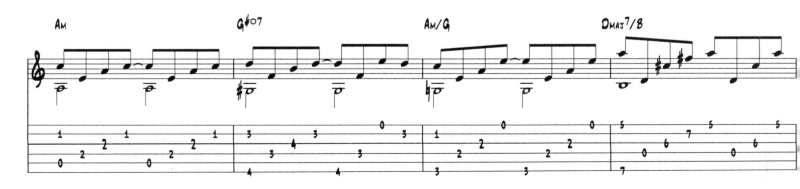